92 Years-
THE POEMS OF MY LIFE

Ruby Pearl Boor Barraw

Order this book online at www.trafford.com
or email orders@trafford.com

Most Trafford titles are also available at major online book retailers.

Printed in the United States of America.

ISBN: 978-1-4669-6870-7 (sc)
ISBN: 978-1-4669-6869-1 (e)

Trafford rev. 09/10/2013

 www.trafford.com

North America & international
toll-free: 1 888 232 4444 (USA & Canada)
fax: 812 355 4082

This book is dedicated, first and foremost, to
my Lord and Savior, Jesus Christ.

To my seven daughters and two sons, all my grand, great
and great-great-grandchildren out of a heart of love.

And to my granddaughter, Lisa, for helping make
the dream of publishing my poems come true.

First Poem

(First poem written in 9th grade at Foch Intermediate High School—
Detroit, Michigan—sitting in art class, looking out the window.)

I like to sit and watch the rain,

As it falls upon the pane,

See people running to and fro,

As they scamper, as they go.

By Ruby Pearl Walkley

*(Grandma never wrote this poem down; she remembered
it all these years. I wrote it down as she told it to me—
Lisa Souder Scarborough, September 3, 1995)*

My Wonderful Tribe

"Wow!" they say. "Eight Children? What a Tribe!"
For you see, I, their mother cannot deny,
That years ago, I'd have thought that a lie.

To think I'd have that many plants
Around my table, while by chance,
Others fate had passed them by,
While they did live the same as I.

They looked at me with scornful eye,
Some made remarks, and they did say:
"How many more before you stop?
You've years to go yet, you sap!"

And I'll admit each time I'd think "Nay, Nay."
But, oh! The joy when they did come,
And took their places within my heart.
They could not know how good it was
As each sweet babe to us was sent,
As we did draw the closer too.

Also my Heavenly Father knew,
I loved Him more and more each day,
As others He sent for me to show The Way.
And teach to them of His great love,
As sharing our blessings from above.

I thank Him for each and every one,
An individual, so different they.
Yet each one shares an equal place,
While I thank God for His great grace,
And truly feel it's worth the race . . .
For now there's nine in any case.

Composed by Mrs. Ruby Boor
Written in 1960 or 1961

I wrote this when I had eight, so the last line was
added later—Dianna came along in 1962.

The Walkley Clan

(Sung to the tune of "I'm so glad I'm a part of the Family of God"
by Bill & Gloria Gaither)

We're so glad we're a part of the Walkley Clan.
We've been raised by the best and forever we'll stand.
We celebrate with loved ones and friends every year.
Good food we all eat, till it comes out our ears.

We're so glad we're a part of the Walkley Clan.
We come here every year from all over the land.
We bring our new-marrieds and our grandchildren too.
We greet everybody with a "how do you do?"

We're so glad we're a part of the Walkley tribe.
Our Indian heritage makes our hearts swell with pride.
We laugh, we cry, and we even have prayer.
There's nothing in this world that we Walkleys can't share.

We remember our loved ones who have gone on before,
Someday we'll be together on that Heavenly shore.
Once you've met a Walkley you're no stranger here.
So come to the reunion, year after year.

By Ruby Boor Barraw & Children
August 1994

Trials Bring Perfecting

Oh that Jesus would come and end it all,
At the time that I feel so close to His call,
But the harder I try and the closer I get,
Tho' the spirit is willing, yet the flesh is so weak.

The devil sure works overtime it doth seem,
And tries extra hard to shatter my dream,
At the time that I feel so wonderfully clean,
Is just the time that he is so mean.

By stirring me up by worry and such,
He makes me hurt those that I love so much.
For being discouraged and sorely depressed,
Not only affects me, but surely the rest.

And family and friends, oh, what a shame,
That even in church the foe has much fame.
Who knows why God's people of the devil are used?
Just what would we do if we were in their shoes?

Remember Job, how that God did allow,
And permit old Satan to turn about,
And take from Job all but his life.
A lesson for all just alike,
For Job remarked, verse twenty, chapter number nine,
To justify myself would condemn this mouth of mine.
Or to say I'm perfect would prove me perverse.
Even so he repented in later verse.

The thought from Job is very plain.
Don't think yourself perfect, or all is vain.
But strive to do God's perfect will.
And through Christ He'll keep perfecting still.

Written by Ruby Boor

April 10, 1995

I'm a mother of nine,
And i think that's fine.
There's Carol, Virginia, Gerald, David, Margaret, Vickie, Lou, Sue
    and Dianna.

I've written one poem already about "my wonderful tribe."
This one now comes more than thirty years later.
Nine beautiful children,
God gave to me.
Each one unique in their own way
And very dear to each other, i must say.

The Eugene Boor family tribe is like no other,
As far as I can tell, for I'm their mother.
All beautiful people, and that's no lie.
Carol has four, and eight grandchildren too
Virginia has two, and a grandchild to boot.
Gerald has two, too young to woo.
David—just one; and he's a step-grandpa too.
Margaret has three, that fills me with glee.
Vickie has four, and Lauren hopes for more.
Lou is still hoping; and Sue has two.
Dianna has three, and a grand-baby.

Written by Ruby Boor Barraw

Twins

I always wanted to have twins, you see.
And I was already a grandma when God brought it to be.
Lou Ann and Sue Ann were aunts as soon as they were born.
On that happy April morn.

Lou Ann came first, they called her twin A,
For they knew Sue Ann, twin B, was on the way.
Quite unusual they were right from the start,
Full-term babies, mom with thirty pounds did part.

They weighed in with less than half that amount.
Thirteen pounds, twelve ounces was the count.
Lou soon grew just a little taller,
While sue was just a little smaller.

Pretty much the same size, they remained
For quite awhile except for their feet.
Their charm and beauty could not be beat.

We thought they would not be nicknamed,
But that proved untrue,
For other names came along too.
There was Bridget for Lou and Midget for Sue.
Also Louie & Suie to boot.

They dressed alike for many years
Receiving from friends many cheers.
They've always been close,
And I want to boast.
I love having twins along with the rest.
Truly, I have really been blessed.

Written by Ruby Boor

Time is Short

Time is short, there is evil all about
And He'll soon be coming with a shout.

We've work to do before the end, my friend,
And sometimes we have to bend.

He's coming for the ones who love—
Not the ones who shove—

Discord and hurt go out the door—
When Jesus enters in once more.

Work for the night will soon be here,
And with our Lord we need not fear.

Written by Ruby Boor
Sabbath morning, November 28, 1992,
from 7:07 to 7:12 AM.

Clara Lou

There's six of us, all older than she;
Then of course, Mother & Dad who brought her to be.
To start with the oldest, there's Alvin you see,
Then Nettie and Lillian, the Twins and then me.

We were all so happy the day she was born,
A beautiful doll, that January morn.
She cooed, and she laughed,
She squeaked, but seldom cried—
How could she, with some one always beside?

Seems she grew up so fast, as our love daily grew;
But spoil her—NO—She was always true blue.
She was always so good, never wanted to fight.
No matter if she was wrong or right.

A lovelier bride you never did see,
As now a handsome hubby belongs to she.
Now they are gone far over the sea,
And some good news of a wee one to be.

We all love each other,
As brothers & sisters should do,
But know that we all feel this same way too.
And do not mind repeating and saying anew,
That to us, just somewhat special she is to our group.

So often we miss her, and tears come to our eyes,
But we look up above and know Thou art nigh;
To keep her safe, and bring her back home to us someday.
Oh, Father in Heaven, we humbly pray.

**Written by Ruby Boor—May, 1956
for Clara Lou (Walkley) Decker**

Prayer is the Answer

Are you tired and weary from the cares of the day?
Heartsick and lonely, then you need to pray.

Friends and loved ones failed you?
Misunderstood what you say?
Put stumbling blocks in your way?
Then you need to pray.

Are you heavy-laden, and need rest for the day?
Come unto Me, Jesus did say.
And you want His presence?
Then you need to pray.

Have you been hurt? Just think of our Lord.
For He did not exert; He took time to pray.

Have you trusted the Father as much as you should?
And read the Bible whenever you could?
Then you need to pray.
Prayer is the answer, the key for the day.
If the Kingdom we enter,
Here . . . we will have to pray.

Composed by Ruby Boor
1970

My Savior's Love For Me is Great

My Savior's love for me is great
So great, you cannot know.
Just what He means to me today.
Oh, I love Him so.

He stooped and lifted me from sin,
From sorrow and from woe,
I had misused His Holy Name,
In deed and thought, you know.

Born and raised in the "Church of God,"
God's commands, I thought I'd kept.
Until one day my heart was pierced,
With all of my neglect.

I realized now, without a doubt,
To Him I must repent.
Be born again, He made me see.
For mother's love, oh, so great—
It could not save me.

Sometimes wrongly judged are we,
Human nature beckoning us to say,
"Oh, what's the use—we just as well may,"
But then the thought comes to me—
God forgives, and so we must.

My Savior's love for me is great;
And I want you to know.
That He's my Judge, my King, My ALL,
Oh, I love Him so!

Written by Ruby Boor in 1957 or 1958
(at the time we were having church on Harper Avenue, just
before we bought John R Church)

To My Other Dad

I want to forget the past
And enjoy the future
I know I was a brat
And don't want to be like I "you-ster."

I know I caused a lot of pain,
For which I am ashamed
I am thankful now
For what you've done for my mom.

And I'd like to be like a son
Please forgive and let's try again.
I want to forget the past
And enjoy the future.

Written by Ruby Boor (for her grandson about his step-dad)

Jefferson-Chalmers Community

Jefferson-Chalmers Community is a nice place
to live, and I wouldn't tell you no fib.
We have been here for thirty-seven years, and
I'll tell you that with very few fears.

But things have changed recently, you know,
and we are all going to be on our toes.
There are a few crooks and hoodlums running around
loose, and we are all ready now to cook their goose.

The mayor has agreed that we are to protect our
property, and to be prepared for prowlers is our right;
We are stepping up our Block Clubs and Neighborhood
Watch—more good citizens are ready to talk and act.

Most people are friendly, thoughtful and good;
and act the way that neighbors should,
But you few hoodlums had better mend your ways.

The Good Book in Proverbs says—
The wicked shall be cut off from the earth,
and the sinners shall be rooted out.
It also says the curse of the Lord is in the house of the
wicked, but He blesseth the habitation of the just.
You thugs beware, you are on your way out. The
good moral people are ready to shout!

We are up in arms and don't intend to take it—
Stop, you thugs, or you may end up where they did.
We want to keep this area what it used
to be, a nice part of the city,
On the Southeast side of Jeff, with trees
and parks and a lot of water yet.

It's cooler down here on the South side of Jeff, and I
often see from my window what the fishermen catch.
There are many stores and businesses, any kind you may need,
And soon to come—Perry's, Farmer Jack and Wendy's to feed.

And churches and schools where they plant good seed.
We have C.D.C., the Mini Station too, and
police patrolling now, quite a few.
The helicopters in the air, and the phone calling
with other block citizens we share.

Bus transportation is close, or a nice walk to Jeff,
or go downtown, twenty minutes or less.
There are all types of people who reside here,
several have been here for many a year.

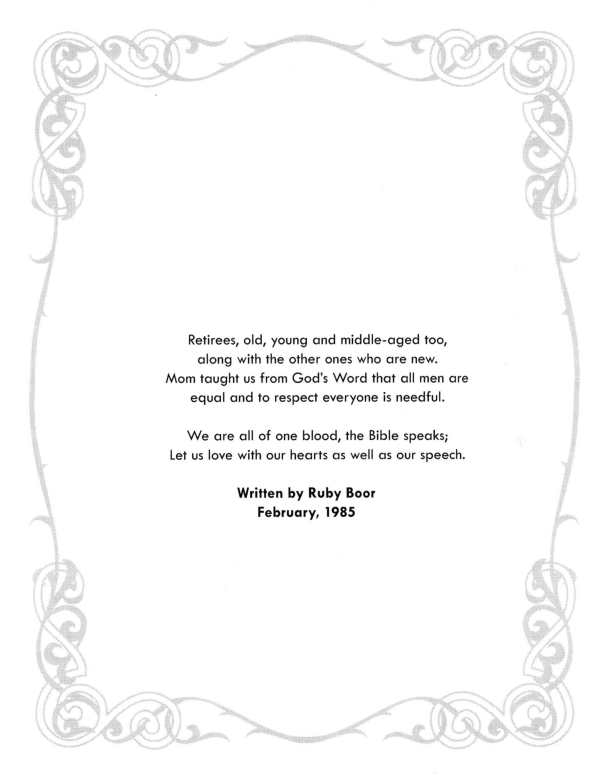

Retirees, old, young and middle-aged too,
along with the other ones who are new.
Mom taught us from God's Word that all men are
equal and to respect everyone is needful.

We are all of one blood, the Bible speaks;
Let us love with our hearts as well as our speech.

Written by Ruby Boor
February, 1985

A Teacher Grand

I often think of a teacher grand,
For I know she has many fans.
She has been at Guyton for many years,
And for this, I want to give three cheers.

All of my children have been taught by her,
Everyone from the last to the first.
She knew how to keep order, yet there was fun,
And also gave home work to everyone.

She was always there for conference day,
And didn't mince words with what she had to say.
They all soon knew that in her room they had to work,
And from their studies they could not shirk.

She was switched around from class to class,
No matter which, she was the best!
Preparing students to take the test,
To enter high school with the rest.

She not only taught well—
The basic Three R's and Truth,
But also about life, love and living,
Give her credit to boot.

Mrs. Tisdall, you have earned your vacation,
And you are still a sensation.
You have met the requirements,
Relax and enjoy your retirement.

With God's blessing, peace, contentment and joy . . .
We are proud of you.

Composed by Ruby Boor
June, 1980 or 1981

My Friend, Millie

I often think of a Lady Grand,
One who had a heart of gold.
So many on her did depend.
She will be missed, to no end.

I've known her for several years.
And both having several children,
We shed some tears.
There were ups and down, good times and bad,
But most the time, we were really glad.

Fun times were always had.
With showers and weddings and babies galore—
No better cook could you find,
And what a joy with her to dine.

The times that I remember the most,
And about Millie, I would like to boast.
We did not talk about denominations, church or Mass,
Or that living right was an easy task.

She spoke of Jesus, the Only One,
And that to Him, alone, everyone should come.
She would call on the phone, and ask me to pray,
And join in for Him to show us the way.

She would ask me to sing, also join in,
And we would sing, "What a Friend We Have in Jesus,"
And, "How Great Thou Art," and "Jesus Is the Only Way."

I'm looking forward to that day, when Jesus comes back in the
    clouds of Heaven to claim His own;
And I will meet my friend, Millie, where we will never part.

We feel that Millie left us too soon—But our consolation is
    the Scripture—Isaiah 57:1 which states this: "The righteous
    perisheth, and no man layeth it to heart, and merciful men are
    taken, none considering that the righteous is taken away from
    the evil to come."

Written by Ruby Boor
July 20, 1991

The Mail Man

I often think of a mail man, grand.
He nods, or smiles, or gives a wave of the hand.
Come rain or shine, he is always there,
As for your mail, you know he cares.

The walking is not all that he has to do,
Do you know that he has to sort it too?
There's Tom, Dick & Harry, Mary and Mike,
He has to make sure the address is right.

There's papers, and books & magazines too,
And also the checks he delivers to you.

He has to watch out for unruly dogs,
Some follow along, maybe two or more.

And the ones in the house know when he's at the door,
There're crooks following after him too, you know,
And they shall be put where good folks don't go.
So appreciate your Mail Man, and pray for him too.
If anyone deserves credit, to him, it is certainly due.

Written by Ruby Boor, 1985

Skipper

I have a little dog and his name is Skipper
But my mom said, it should have been Yipper
He barks all the time; and on his mouth needs a zipper,
He eats from a dish and drinks from a dipper.

He plays with the cat and is quite a flipper
He grabs the cat's food and is a gypper
He romps and plays and acts like a nipper
His hair is short, so he needs no clipper.

And he likes to run away with your slipper
He won't let it go and sure is a gripper
He dances on his hind legs, oh what a hipper
He even smiles, look at that lipper.

What a cute pup, he is a pipper
And he makes a mess, oh my, what a ripper
He likes ice cream and he is a sipper
And this poem was written by my mom, the quipper.

Composed by Ruby Boor

Darlene, "My Big Beautiful Doll"

She is taller than me, you see.
But yet she looks up to me.

Grafted into "Our Family Tree,"
A sister to one and all,
One on whom, we all can call,
And she's always "on the ball."

She volunteers to help at church,
Arlie had said, she sure does work—
You'd think she has several hands,
I know that she has many fans.

She is talented in many ways you see,
And God's praises, she sings with glee.
There for our family, Arlie loved her too
Having eight girls, makes one coo.

Darlene, I want to give you a toast,
For I want to boast, "I see Jesus in you,"
The song I love to hear you sing the most.

Written by Ruby Boor
for Darlene Wibby Ali
April 8, 1995—Happy Birthday, My Girl-from Mom B.

Saul Turned Paul

Saul cussed and swore as he went out the door
Jumped in his car, and pushed the gas to the floor
He zoomed down the street, not caring which way,
Nor bothering to heed the signs on the way.

He traveled right on and through the stop street.
And soon what he heard was a loud, tweet—tweet.
The officer motioned for him to park,
And gave him the summons to appear in court.

The judge sat on the bench, as he stepped to the stand.
"I'm guilty, your honor, I've been a bad man.
I've not cared about others, nor did I obey,
The laws of the land, based on God's 10 commands—Forgive me,
    your honor—I repent today,
For in this jail, I do not want to stay."

The judge looked **Paul** over—saw tears in his eyes,
And spoke with compassion, as he did rise,
"You're free to go—no longer under the law,
But go with grace, if you will keep the right pace."

Written February 2, 1969 by Ruby Boor

27

Grace

I often think of a Lady Grand
And I want to give her a hand.
From the first time I met her,
I was one of her fans.

Arlie said she was a peach
And he wanted us to meet.
She was always so friendly
And light-hearted too.
You just knew she was true blue.

A wonderful cook, Arlie loved her food.
She always put us in a good mood.
Delicious meat, and vegetables too,
She just couldn't give enough to you.

Pies are her specialty, and her omelets just great.
Yes, she bakes bread too, along with cake.
The food was scrumptious, but the best part of all,
Was knowing she was someone on whom you could call.

Always so cheerful, she just makes your day,
Our love for her will ever stay.
It's always so neat to hear Grace pray,
Thanking God for our blessings today.

Grant also was special—so meek, gentle and kind.
He must have had a brilliant mind.
And for many a year, he and Arlie had a good time.

We miss all our loved ones who've gone on before.
But some day we will all meet at that beautiful door
And Grace will be cooking for us some more.

Composed by Ruby Boor for Grace Harold—May, 1995

Lillian Parke

We nominate a lady grand,
For she has many fans.
Well known and liked by all,
She's well-versed and on the ball.

Mother of eight, all in school,
She volunteers there as a rule.
Having been active in many a group,
She knows quite well how to cope.

Smooths things over, between many folk.
She's well-educated and in the know,
Full of spark, Lillian Parke.
We give you our vote.

Written by Ruby Boor

Membership Drive

Come one, come all,
Please heed the call,
Parents, friends and teachers,
Let's get on the ball.

Everyone is needed—
No one excluded,
Let's show our administrators
That they are appreciated.

Mr. Washington, our Principal, is a fine man.
In fact, we all think that he is grand.
Mrs. Simowski is everyone's pal.
So, she too, is quite a gal.

Our teachers too, are in the groove,
So come on friends, let's move.
So join the group, let's all agree,
That happy people we can be.

Composed by Ruby Boor
for Membership Drive PTO October 22-Nov. 12, 19____

Baby Shower

Mommy's expecting, and we think that's great.
Daddy's so happy, he takes the cake.
They are beaming all over, and they surely do rate.
Grandma & Grandpa and others too,
Quite a few that does make.

But no stuff for the baby, for goodness sake.
Our baby things are worn out, or given away.
Let's have a party! What do you say?
There'll be fun and prizes and good food too.
We hope that we can count on you.
Come along and join us too.

Composed by Ruby Boor

Doctor Lepley

I often think of that doctor of mine,
And thank you, Dear Lord, for that man of Thine,
For on him you've bestowed that wonderful gift,
Of knowing just how to restore the sick.

He's treated the whole family,
Mother & Daddy, down to their children's babes,
And all of us have said,
That we would never our doctor trade.

He's jolly and full of laughter,
He's meek, kind and gentle—Yet strong and sure.
What more could you ask when expecting a cure?

Not a bit old-fashioned although he makes sure
of these modern devices,
And knows just what to do in case of a crisis.

Whether it's skin disease, fractures or bruises,
maternity, operations or broken bones,
I think he's just tops that doctor of our home.

I could write on and on if I was a poet—
For it's in my heart, but no words can show it.
But to FRED O. LEPLEY, I say today,
That I think you're swell in every way.

Written by Ruby Boor for Dr. Lepley in 1953

David

(Proverbs 3:1-12)

Dear David,

I'm wondering how you are, As I lie here in the dark,
Asking where I failed with you and just when did it start.
I was so glad, that June morn, the day that you were born—
My fourth child, my second son,
Two girls and two boys to us had come.
Named David, suggested by Grandma,
And dedicated to the Lord—
Came church and Sabbath school, and you learned the rules—
And wrote right answers on the board.
You grew up and liked to roam, hardly ever stayed at home.
Forgot the 10 Commandments, that you'd shown,
Remember when you wrote it on a scroll and put it neatly in a roll.
Dear Son, come back, I pray before that day,
When time runs out, to late to turn about.
Come now, repent on bended knee,
And you'll see our Savior's love is given free.
He'll pardon, bless and help you.
With Him, you cannot fail. He saves to the uttermost,

Without Him, you are lost and to the gutter goest—
Please son, come back, I pray—
For this world is soon to vanish away.
Oh, prepare now for that better day.

<u>(Several years later:)</u>
Dear Son—I came across this poem written many years ago, when you liked to roam. You have been married now for several years, with a fine wife and son to boot. There have been ups and downs, good times and bad, glad times and some that were sad; but just had to finish this poem to let you know that we are glad. For you've started on the right track now, to Orlando.

Composed by Ruby Boor

During The Night

Ofttimes I'm awakened by this or that,
Or the closing of a door, when Lou comes in,
And I thank the Lord once more.

Sometimes it's a siren, or the barking of a dog,
Or a boat whistle in the fog.
Then the night is still,
And these are times I begin to pray.

I am alone with God, and so thankful ever—
That with me He doth stay.
I pray for family and friends and foes
And ask his blessing upon all of those.

The time must be short, there's fear all around;
And everywhere evil abounds.
People care less about each other;
And, at the same time, call them brother.
There's no respect for father and mother,
And parents sometimes hardly bother.

Scripture is being fulfilled, not much time left.
God is putting us through a test.
Please read God's Word and daily pray,
Or from His love you will surely stray.

Composed by Ruby Boor
During night—August 29—3:00-4:00 AM (Year: _____?)

"The Doctors Grand"

I often think of "the doctors grand"—
As I lie here in my hospital room.
Knowing too, that they'll be coming soon,
With a word of cheer, as they dress my wound.
They come walking in, one, or five at a time,
And hurrying out after spending some time.
Some live here, and some go away,
But there is always plenty on hand for the day.
All sizes and ages—they don't look alike,
But you'll find they confer on just what's right.
They stroll down the hall, as they talk, this and that,
And you know too, that they'll soon by back.
To give an injection, if you are in pain,
And before very long, you are not the same.
They baby you, when it need be,
But then when it's time, they know just what to do.
The stitches are cut, and all tubes gone out,
And before long you're happy to be about.
Being back home to family and friends too,
And thanking God, for all he permits,
The "Grand Doctors" to do.
So to Henry Ford Hospital, I say, Thank-You;
And will always remember all that you do,
And especially thank God for all the "Grand Doctors" too.

Written by Ruby Boor

June 10, 1971 at Ford Hospital, when I was operated on by
Dr. Ponka for gall bladder—Written in appreciation for all
the doctors of Henry Ford Hospital and especially dedicated
to Dr. Ponka, Dr. Hays, Dr. Lee, Dr. Cromwell, Dr. Dallolma,
Dr. Murphy, Dr. Turro and Dr. Jung. (I wrote that on top of
each copy I presented to the doctors. Dr. Ponka + 7 doctors
under him)—Note: See poem, "The Doctors Grand—Part 2"

"The Doctors Grand—Part 2"

I often think of "the doctors grand,"
As I am here again in my hospital room.
I'm getting wets and soaks, and creams galore,
And still my body itches for more.
It feels so good in that wet—with the plastic wrap,
That I'll soon be able to take a nap.
The nurses and doctors are all so kind,
Maybe I won't lose my mind.
There are others here too—who are worse than me—
I pray that they, too, from the rash—will soon be free.
Ford Hospital is great—and the patients still rate,
But it is not long until they give you the gate.
They still come by one or several at a time,
And their orders you should mind,
And I claim them all as doctors of mine.
But there's one special guy, I've known more than 21 years—
And with Dr. Beninson, I have no fears.
I thank you, God, for that man of thine,
And I pray for him all the time.
So to Henry Ford Hospital I again say thank you;
And especially thank God for all he permits
"the grand doctors" to do.

Written by Ruby Boor, April 8, 1983

Vickie Lynn

V	is for **V**ictorious—that's her goal;
I	is for **I**nward—a beautiful soul.
C	is for **C**hristian—she'll always be.
K	is for **K**indness to all she sees.
I	is for **I**deal, as mother, daughter and wife.
E	is for **E**xotic and so full of life.
L	is for **L**oving; she's everyone's friend;
Y	is for **Y**ielding; she listens too.
NN	is for **N**o **N**onsense—She's always true blue.
	Such a beautiful daughter—
	And I'm so glad that she's mine.

Written by Ruby P. Boor Barraw
from Mother—to Vickie

My Number Two Girl

My girl is fifty, number two along the line,
And she gets sweeter and sweeter all the time.
She's always been tops in her class,
A smart girl, she is quite a lass.

She's kind and gentle, yet takes no sass.
She sticks up for the right, without a fight.
Nicely putting you in place, so sit tight.

She has much love for family and friends,
And world affairs she knows too.
But most of all is her relationship with God,
And her fellow man—And when she prays for you,
You know you're on the mend.

She's talented too in many ways—
Piano, song and hospitality;
For she cares for you and me and wants us all
Our Heavenly Father to see.

So, Virginia is fifty, isn't that nifty?
She still is spiffy, and that's not iffy.
She's quite a lady, always read in a jiffy;
To help someone, or offer a prayer
And you know that the Lord has heard her quickly.
She's always been a smart person—her mind works swiftly;
And never is shifty. So, if you all agree, just give her fifty.
(Claps that is.)

Written by Ruby Boor Barraw / June, 1992

My Number Two Girl (# 2)

Virginia is number two along my line,
And she gets sweeter and sweeter all the time.
She's always been tops in her class,
A smart girl, she is quite a lass.
She's kind and gentle, yet takes no sass.
She sticks up for the right, without a fight,
Nicely putting you in place, so sit tight.

She has much love for family and friends,
And world affairs she knows too.
But most of all is her relationship with God
And her fellow man.
And when she prays for you,
You know you're on the mend.
She talented too in many ways—
Piano, song and hospitality.

For she cares for you and me and wants us all
Our Heavenly Father to see.
She still is spiffy, and that's not iffy.
She's quite a lady, always read in a jiffy.
To help someone, or offer a prayer
And you know that the Lord has heard her prayer.

She's always been a smart person
And worked at Clintondale School System,
Where God had it planned to meet that special man,
The High School principal, right up her alley,
Here was more than her equal, two brainy people.
We were overjoyed when Ginny married Dave,
This wonderful man, who became part of our clan.
This marriage brought Ginny some beautiful daughters, and to
    David some fine sons, and now all those grand children give
    them so much fun.

**<u>Written by Ruby Boor Barraw / May 2010 in honor
of Dave and Ginny's 25th Wedding Anniversary</u>**

El Dean and Carol

I often think of a couple grand,
A pretty girl, and a handsome man.
They have been together for several moons,
And their eyes light up when one enters the room.
To them was born three girls and a boy;
And now three grand-children are their joy.
There's Bryan, Cheryl, Lisa and Tammy,
Melissa, Sabriena and Sammy.
Not in that order, but words are handy;
And I think that's dandy.
God has always come first in their home.
They always paid tithe and offering too;
And to the Church of God remain true,
And never any outstanding bills due.
They are fun to be with, laughter and jokes.
Even if nonsense gets your goat.
She flirts a lot, and he gives friendly pokes.
Yet their love for each other is the most.
So for 25 years we make this toast.
To El Dean & Carol Souder, we say today.
Your Marriage is here to stay,
Until the day, God calls us away.

Written by Ruby Boor, March 1983

Dear Father, I thank Thee for the night's rest,
While Thou didst watch over all the rest,
Of neighbors, friends and loved ones dear,
Along with all of the family here.
We thank You for providing food and clothes,
And asking for help to share with those,
Who less fortunate may be,
That we might help them too, you see,
To look to Thee and thankful be,
That sons and daughters, we all are of Thee.

Written by Ruby Boor

Oh! Love of God, it is so great, He even included me,
I am so glad with Him, I'd rate, the same as you or she.
To me, He is my very best friend, on Him I will rely.
He took me in, saved me from sin, His promises are mine.

As long as I will do His will, I know that He doth bless,
Our home with love and perfect peace while leaning on His breast.
And when at times my thoughts may stray away from Heavenly things,
He speaks to me and gently says, "This is not right, you see.

Rebuke Old Satan and he will fleet—that I have promised thee.
Cast on Me your every care and trust in My great grace.
Come unto Me, I'll give you rest and peace & joy within.
I'll fill your soul and make you free; the truth is plain to see.

If you would live, abide with Me and My commandments keep.
As I have said all through my Word and many still repeat.
I loved you first, before you knew—and now 'tis up to you,
For whosoever will may come; and that includes you too."

Written by Ruby Boor

Jason E. Hammer

You are sixteen now, a handsome young man.
We all love you, so take a bow.
Getting a car, you are blessed—
Keeping that car will be the test.
That piece of machinery can give you joy,
If you use it wisely and not as a toy.

You must still go to school, and obey the rules,
And Don't hang around with fools.
Drivers training you must pass
To be in the right class.

You must honor your elders,
<u>They do give good advice.</u>
Remember this or you will think twice.
Don't let anyone say, "I told you so."
You be the one good behavior to show.

There's gas to buy and insurance to pay,
And it takes money to keep it on its way.
First comes school, and then there's work,
And if you don't know this, your duties you shirk,
(or **you** are a jerk),
If you will do this, you will be blessed,
A clever young man, YES.
  By Grandma B, who loves you very much, November 30, 1990

R   is for Rachel—a Sweet Personality;

A   is for Attainment—She will reach her goal, you see

C   is for Courageous—She will get her degree

H   is for Head—She will be at the top

E   is for Eternal—She will get that life

L   is for Logic—Everything will turn out all right

Put them all together, they spell **RACHEL**,
A word that means the world to me.

**By Grandma B., July 28, 1995 for August 5th Birthday for
Rachel Hoaglund (Appleby)**

Matthew

M   is for Matthew—he is just tops

A   s for anchor—he is a solid rock

T   s for touching—he gives good back rubs

T   is for talent and in him you can trust

H   is for heart—he is caring

E   is for energy—he's helpful and sharing

W   is for worth—he trods the right turf

**Written by Grandma Ruby Boor Barraw
for Matthew Hoaglund (Appleby)**

Please Be On Time!

The time is set for 2 o'clock
Not at four or six
So be on time—don't dawdle
For dinner we will fix.

Not only family, we are friends
And owe this courtesy
So be on time, your dish in hand
And happy we will be.

When we eat, we would like
All the food in place
So if you're late, it won't be good
And we'll get on your case!

**Composed by Ruby Boor & daughter Virginia
This little poem was included in an invitation to a family
gathering of some kind.**

Volunteers for Saratoga

Garasa—That's the place to go,
This hospital, now, is one of the best, you know.
It has been enlarged, improved and added on, we want to boast.
Parking is free, and a new wing for the elderly is the most.

In Bulk Mail we have lots of fun,
And we stuff, button and label as we sit around the table.
There are stacks of papers and envelopes galore—Never time to
    get bored.

You can hear Marian's laugh all over the place, as everyone gets on
    Jerry's case.
Millie is the chief and is real sweet,
And Ellie's sense of humor can't be beat.

Beverly, Sharon, Kathy and Diane drop in and chat for awhile,
And soon for the mail bags we have quite a pile.
Nick and Jean are fun people too,
And as I am new here, I can only mention a few.

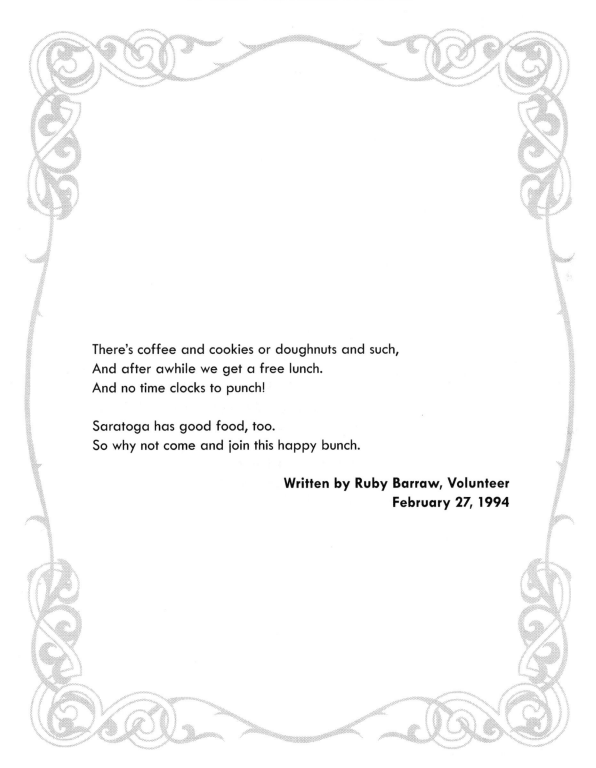

There's coffee and cookies or doughnuts and such,
And after awhile we get a free lunch.
And no time clocks to punch!

Saratoga has good food, too.
So why not come and join this happy bunch.

Written by Ruby Barraw, Volunteer
February 27, 1994

Baby Shower

Everyone knows it should not have happened,
but it did.
Dianna was a wreck, and **Ron** blew his lid.
Jennifer couldn't believe it and neither could **Mike**.
Abortion was wrong, adoption—for them, not right.
Friends and teachers understood,
Showing Godly compassion, in this hour.
Scripture says, "Children are an heritage of the Lord."
We now take off the fetters and will rejoice.

By Grandma Ruby Boor Barraw

"Another Teacher Grand"

I often think of "A Teacher Grand"
For I know that he has many fans.
Not only his homeroom, but he is loved by all;
He is really on—that is on the ball.

He is firm, yet gentle, he is strict but kind,
No monkey business with him, you'll find.
He must love children, one and all,
For on him even the wee ones do call.

They, too, can't wait to be in his room
Where all the kids think the time does zoom.
They work first, and then they play
So all are ready for another day.

The contests go on between his sections—
Children being urged on toward perfection.
The kids come home all aglow,
Telling parents how things did go.

Greenfield Village is his special treat,
And a better leader you'll never meet.
He plans picnics, outings, and such.

A good example to all of us,
As before the meal he pauses to say,
"Will someone volunteer to ask
Blessing on the food today?"

He's active in Scouts and P.T.A.,
Never too busy to help in some way.
So to Mr. Weitschat we say today,
"Truly you are 'A Teacher Grand'
And we all want to give you a hand,
For we thank God for such a man."

By Ruby Boor

She is our Grandma Mother

Written by Marilyn Anderson (Brown)
(3/31/1942 to 10/15/1981)

She is our Grandma Mother,
It is her who taught us fear.
And for us there can be no other.
'Twas her that brought us here.

She is our Grandma Mother,
You can be sure of that.
With love that couldn't be measured.
For who'd know where the beginning was at.
"'Tis her love we've all shared and treasured.
She is our Grandma Mother.

Grandma has always been there.
And our troubles she's gladly shared.
But were we afraid or gently swayed.
She'd get on her knees in prayer.

From Grandma Mother we all have learned
For she is our family rock.
When necessary, she is stern,
But her love, it has no lock.
Tho' her hand was oh, so firm,
On her door, anyone could knock.

Nobody knows what to say,
"tho we sure have tried in every way,
To say what it means to us,
To have a Grandma Mother,
Who makes such a fuss over us.

And to one man, she has given a wonderful life,
Although there has been some sorrow and strife.
For you see, our Grandma Mother,
Is our own Papa's loving wife.

Though gentle are they, as anyone will say.
When we were down, they lifted our frown.
And if we were lost, they shared the cost.
For it a wound we did have, Grandma
Would say, "Get the Petro Carbo salve."

If some don't, they sure oughta have,
Two parents, like our Mom and Dad.
Harry & Pearl gave us the name,
That started everyone talking.
For you see, theirs wasn't the same
As that wonderful family of "Walkley."

Mother, Great and Grand

To: Grandma Walkley (Pearl Walkley) From: Virginia Lee Boor

You've heard of family matriarchs—
The mother of the clan.
Well, our family has one also,
According to His plan.

But ours is not a Ruler,
In the sense you might have guessed.
Nonetheless, she is the leader.
Having her, we all are blessed.

For she has so much wisdom,
Compassion, and great love.
Her whole life is devoted,
To our Father up above.

How many times, in need herself,
Of some material thing,
She thinks first of others,
A helping hand to bring.

Raising seven children of her own,
Was not an easy chore.
But no other mother's children,
Could love their mother more.

No, she hasn't had an easy life,
Some days, worked from dawn 'til dusk
Cows to milk, chickens to feed,
And then, the corn to husk.

Not to mention making jellies,
Pickles, pies and cake,
And all the other goodies,
Our mother likes to make.

Not only is she "Mother"—
She grand-mothers quite a few.
And they love her dearly,
Thirty-five grandchildren do!

To others, she's great-grandma,
Twenty-nine to be precise.
Some are too young know,
They've a great-grandma who's so nice.

Yes, there's a mother of our clan.
She's great and grand-ma too.
But all her "children" love her,
For the mother of the clan is <u>YOU!</u>

Happy Anniversary

To: Mother and Dad From: Virginia Lee (1966)

Twenty-nine years of wedded bliss,
Well, not always with <u>everything</u> right!
Sometimes they had quarrels
And the budget was tight.

But who in this world could ever imply
That Ruby Pearl Walkley chose the wrong guy?
He was "the one," she knew from the start
She'd love her Gene with all her heart.

And so they were married; "No kids, he did say.
"I like other people's children, let's keep it that way!"
But alas! there came Carol, as sweet as could be
And then (West) Virginia, her middle name's Lee.

Then came Gerald, first-born son,
And then "King" David, the "mis-cha-vous" one.
Two boys and two girls, a perfect fam-i-ly
But there was more to add to their "tree."

Margaret arrived in March of '53.
Followed by another, named Vick-ie.
How many times we heard her say,
this familiar old cliche:
"What's sweeter than a baby? Two Babies" . . . Yessireee . . .

So guess what happened late one night?
Two babies were born. Yes, you're right.
Lou and Sue, and how they sang
And they said they ended up with a bang!

There was just one more, your hearts to win
A sweet little girl named Dianna Lynn.
Which added up to the sum of nine
And don't you think it turned out fine?

My Mom

She's hard to describe—this mother of mine.
There are lots of words, by which to define,
But none could do justice, or say enough—
To portray her goodness and just the "right stuff."

She's friendly and kind, compassionate too,
Ready to serve—it matters not who.
Always willing to help—no need to ask,
She'll share her belongings and help with your task.

She'll sing a hymn in the last moments of life,
To comfort a dying man and also his wife.
Trusts in the Lord—"Nothing's Impossible," she'll say;
And she's helped so many to find **The Way**.

Always stands up for what she knows is right;
Some of her Grandchildren call her, "Dyn-O-Mite!"
The mother of nine—she's true blue to the core,
She's Grandma, Great-Grandma, Aunt Ruby, and more!

There are others, not even related who call her "mom" too.
"Always room for one more," she claims quite a few.
Out rolls the "red carpet," when you walk through her door,
She feeds you and cheers you and offers you more.

She volunteers at the hospital, Saratoga by name,
And helps in the church, but not for the fame.
Married at sixteen—to Eugene a good wife—
And after he passed, she still had so much life.

So Arlie, she wed—Valentine's Day, '88
They shared almost five years that were just great!
And when he, like Gene, went to be with the Lord,
She mourned the loss, but knew the Reward.

"We don't sorrow as others who have no hope."
Although at times, it was hard to cope.
But she reached out to others with troubles and cares,
Putting aside her own problems and snares.

Always encouraging us to trust in the Lord,
There's been many rough waters, she's helped us to ford.
When I think of my mom, I think of a wonderful Mother,
Who has done more to shape my life than any other.

I think of one who's there when I need her the most,
She's the best Mom in the World—I have to boast.
My mom just had a birthday—she turned seventy-three,
And I want her to know how precious she is to me!

I LOVE YOU, MOM
Virginia Lee
October, 1994

Margaret Ann

The first I ever heard of you,
Was months before your birth.
It was more than 14 years ago,
And our hearts were filled with mirth.

I'd mopped the floor that certain day,
And left it sopping wet.
Then ran to watch TV,
So Mom began to fret.

She called me back to finish up;
And as she watched me there,
I grumbled and complained—
I didn't think it fair.

Then, with a twinkle in her eye,
And a look of apprehension.
She started to speak and what she said,
Captivated my attention.

"Do you want me to fall down," she said,
"And hurt your baby sister?"
In surprise, I laughed and cried.
Then I hugged and kissed her.

That's how she broke the news to me,
And I couldn't have been gladder.
After that I knew for sure,
The reason Mom got fatter.

Well, the months went by,
And finally you were born.
And if I'm not mistaken,
It was early in the morn.

We couldn't wait to see you,
Our brand new little girl.
The thought of our own "living doll,"
Put us in a whirl.

Then came the day they brought you home,
I ran out to the car.
Mom let me take you in the house,
'Cause it wasn't very far.

When I picked you up,
I couldn't believe you were there
So small and tiny a bundle
The blankets seemed light as air.

But when I got you safely inside,
And peeked beneath that green shawl,
To my relieved delight,
You were in there, after all.

Hair like silk—black as coal,
A little turned-up nose,
Tiny, fragile and oh so sweet,
And your mouth was like a rose.

What happiness you brought us then,
And all these many years
Through all our ups and down
Amid our joy and tears.

But . . . could we find a better sister?
No! We never can!
To us, you are unique . . .
Our sister, Margaret Ann.

Happy Birthday—from Virginia Lee

Luck or Miracle?

Everyone knows of someone who has experienced it, if not themselves personally. Sometimes we come away from a dangerous situation or near tragedy with surprisingly little or no consequences and wonder how was that possible.

In German it might be called "gluck-im-ungluck" (rhymes with book) and means good-luck-within-misfortune. Of course "wunder" or miracle is also often heard. Especially for those that have faith in a greater power, the latter is not just an off-hand expression. For them, there can be no doubt about the existence of a spiritual guardian or angel. It is for them a natural phenomena. Indeed, there are too many such occurrences among the truly faithful to be brushed off as just luck. Often a call for help is answered with astonishing speed, then again in a more subtle or protective manner, when it is least expected. Here is a recent example of just such a case. Judge for yourself:

A near and dear relative of mine was at the wheel of her car and stopped at a traffic light. Quite suddenly she was jolted from behind. Damage to the car was very slight and the other driver sped off without stopping.

Though not seriously injured, she experienced a sudden sharp pain in her back and her pulse raced. Earlier in the day she had an unusually high pulse rate but did not deem it necessary to see a doctor right away. Now it was more urgent, and so during the initial examination and heart monitoring her heart stopped for eight seconds. She was given a heart pacer which may have been just in the nick of time. Quite possibly, the person who bumped her car from behind inadvertently did her a great service. Was it simply good-luck-within-misfortune or did she have that guardian angel?

Robert Masters, Germany
Son of Lillian & Homer Masters
Nephew of Ruby Boor Barraw—of whom this piece was
written

What Makes Friendships Happen?

What makes friendships happen?
Is it accident or design?
What made this special feeling
Start between your heart and mine?
What special words did we exchange?
Perhaps we'll never know.
Or was it during the quiet hours,
The warmth began to grow?
I like to think our Father knew.
You needed me, as I needed you.
And that the friendship our hearts share,
Is ours because He put it there.
Just want to say how glad I am,
From one day to another,
That somehow in God's special plan
We happened to each other.

By Jean Kyler McManus

Nostalgia . . . by Betty Sexton

We like to recall
The good old days,
When life was so different
In so many ways.

A relationship meant
We got married first,
Then faced life together
Through the best and the worst.

Soft ware kept us warm
On a cold, winter night,
And chips kept the fire
In the stove burning bright.

When fever set in,
We had few doctor bills,
For salves or home-remedies
Cured most of our ills.

Earrings were clip-ons
And won by the girls;
And they, not the boys
Wore their hair in long curls.

The boys wore the pants
And the girls wore the laces;
You could tell which was which
Without seeing their faces.

Diapers were cloth
And were rinsed on the spot,
Not disposed of in cans
Or some parking lot.

Would I want to go back
And live in the past?
I pondered the question
And thought hard and fast.

Nostalgia is nice,
But I'll have to admit
Surrendering some things
Would hurt me a bit.

Cruise control on the road
Makes driving a dream,
And power steering and I
Are a great little team.

I prefer air-conditioning
To fans with the pleats,
And my freezer beats cellars
For storing my eats.

My dryer is handy,
My washer a must—
So I'll just take the present
And try to adjust.
Song For My Mother

What can I say about her?
What can I say that hasn't already been said?
She is my mother; she is my mother;
And I love her, yes I love her.

For she was the one who first told me about God
And she was the one who taught me how to pray.
A debt I owe to this precious mother
It is a debt I never could repay.

When I was young, she taught me right from wrong.
She is a guiding light; she won't give up the fight
To try to do what's right
My precious mother.

I thank God for my mother;
She compares to none other
My precious mother.

By Virginia L. Vogel, September 1996

Margaret Ann

Margaret Ann, my middle one,
And loved just as much as any one.
Her grandmother Walkley came to be with mom,
With message from Marilyn to wait until her birthday which was on
    Tuesday.

She did arrive on that day, on March, thirty-first,
And Marilyn's buttons burst.
Likewise all the rest too—
She was such a little doll,
The smallest of them all.

She was very good in school
And always obeyed the rule.
She graduated before she was eighteen,
Then worked for the clinic, the St. John team.

She was very thrifty, and knew how to save,
And before long, her new car payments were made.
She paid $800, down without a frown,
A good driver she is, all around.

Like her mother, she eloped,
And 'twas later when she spilled the dope.
She got a fine man, along with his clan,
Who are some of the best folks in the land.

Especially his mamma, whom we all love-
Her characteristics are like some one above,
Then there's Aaron and Kevan and Danielle too.
And Margaret is a great mother, to boot.

Read Proverbs 31 and you will see—
That she has many of these.

Written by Ruby Boor Barraw
October 17, 1996

Dianna Lynn

Dianna is my youngest one,
And just like all the rest
A beauty and a lot of fun.

She entered this world, amid an icy storm—
On a January morn,
And spent her first two weeks at Henry Ford.

She was just fine, but mom had caught an infection
So they kept her in a different section.
So cute was she that they used her for the bath demonstration,
Where all the new mothers are taken.

She was so good in school, her friends thought her cool.
She loved her second grade teacher, Miss Madden, who later
    became Mrs. Mermell.
And along with mom and twin sisters she attended her wedding, as
    well.

Her seventh grade teacher taught her so well,
That in the 8th grade she vacationed quite a spell.
She had good friends and did court,
But then along came Ron, that special sport.

That was her guy, and they soon wed.
A beautiful couple everyone said.
She's now a mother of three, and a grandmother of one, Breanna is
    such fun.

Jennifer is in the medical field,
And Jonathan and Jordan may make the big league.
So for this union, we are all pleased.

By Ruby Boor Barraw
November 10, 1996

Doctor Ansaldi

Now, there is another doctor of mine,
And I thank God too, for that "man of thine."
Dr. Ansaldi is his name, and he has such fame.

When my heart raced, he even came to the hospital on a Sunday
And I ended up with a pacemaker on Monday.
For other problems, he usually knows what's wrong before the tests.

Yes, our family thinks, he is one of the best.
A busy man—yet takes time to talk,
And to call you back, he does not balk.

Keep him safe, oh Lord we pray
As you guide him every day.
Bless Nurse Jeanna too, his right arm,
Very capable too, and with much charm.

By Ruby P. Barraw
November 11, 1996

Pastors Jim and Jan Holder

I often think about pastors Jim and Jan
She is a sweetheart—to a wonderful man.
They have been together for many years,
Teaching God's word without any fears.
She is a great teacher, and he, what a preacher!
Fasten your seat belts and hear this:

Pastor Jim knows that God is not deaf—
I think he just wants to make sure that we are paying attention!
He loves to preach from the Old Testament,
Divided by man, not by God,
For that's the same scripture from which Jesus and the disciples taught.
He teaches us about God's love
And if we obey, we will have blessings from above

Our pastors have great faith in God's healing power,
For they have experienced this healing themselves
And know how to pray for the rest.

Pastors are busy people—
They are praying for us all at the crack of dawn.
Sometimes they lose sleep at night,
But never to busy to answer the call,
Praying for your ailments and troubles.

Baptisms, weddings, counselings and funerals—
Don't forget that they also need our prayers
And also our love offerings as they make their trip to Africa (their
    yearly calling)
May they bring souls to the Lord as they expound God's word
But Lord, please bring them back safely to us, we pray

**Written by Ruby P. Barraw, 87 years young, September
20, 2008, mother of Virginia Vogel and Margaret
Saberan, who attend church at New Hope Full Gospel
Church, where Jim and Jan Holder are the pastors)**

Sabriena LeSal

And she is quite a gal,
Beautiful from birth
And always with mirth
Even from the time she was only a little squirt.

Being an only child,
She could have been spoiled,
But being raised in church,
She had many good role models.

Her energy could not be bottled,
Such a sweet spirit,
She cannot be beat—
Everyone loves with her to meet.

Written in June 2002 by Great Grandma Dynomite, Ruby (Boor) Barraw

I Often Think of Bernice . . . (a fine lady)

We have known each other since our children were school age. They all attended Guyton School, which at that time, was one of the best in the nation. Many years we all had there at Guyton—before they entered high school. The teachers were cool and we had one of the best PTA's in town. The favorite was Bill Weitschat, who everyone liked and we had a big celebration when he won teacher of the year.

I think all of you appreciate Bernice's smile and that little laugh and always her sense of humor, a real positive person—never down. She has always been nice to be around. That Jeff-Chalmers area was a beautiful sigh, and the shopping area just right. There was Sutton's Drugs, Kresges, Mushro's Children's Corner, Detroit Edison, churches and banks and Sanders, where we often had lunch. Also on Jefferson, remember the Cinderella Theater, Vanity Ballroom, and the A & P store. The street car tracks and the buses and we went downtown, where there was Hudson's and Kerns with the big clock, Greenfield Cafeteria and more. The big Kresge's and Woolworth's where we had our picture taken and the lunch counters, where we got the good vegetable soup and the waffle ice cream sandwiches, and the kids' clothes and toys were so cheap. Remember too, the Booth Theater, Water Works Park, Belle Isle, the Big Stove, U.S. Rubber, Park-Davis. We went to Greenfield Village and the Detroit Zoo.

There was Electric Park, the Naval Armory, The Whittier and the ferry boat too. And close to us, Lakewood Park, Angel Park and Grosse Pointe Park, swimming pool, where sometimes our kids sneaked in too. The TV came out in our day, yet our clan took time to play. I introeuc3d to to my neighbor and friend, Beverly, and you became good friends and sometimes we still get together—not often enough and time does fly, but I hope and pray we can all be together in the great by-and-by in that beautiful heavenly place, where we will never have to part.

Much love on your 80th birthday, Bernice (Pickert).

**Love,
Ruby Boor Barraw**

Christina Joy

We all loved it when Christina joined our family tree, and truly you
    are a joy, Christina Joy.

That sweet smile just warms our hearts,
And you are so smart
We are amazed at your talents,
You sing and dance, and love to perform,
For your age, you are above the norm.

We love your witty answers and little jokes,
And the way you relate
With all sizes, and ages
Your life is going to be many pages.

Your love for the Lord
shows true blue,
And we all are so thankful that he hears about us from you,
When you remember us in prayer and his many blessings we all
    share.

From Great Grandma Dynomite—almost 91 and now quite a sight
But wait, some day in the kingdom,
We will all have heavenly bodies,
And the Word of God said we shall know as we are known,
And never have to part.

From your Great Grandma Ruby Pearl (Boor) Barraw, who loves you
and my nice big family so much. You have such good parents,
who love you so much.

**Written by Ruby Pearl (Walkley Boor) Barraw, September, 2012,
the day Christina Joy Scarborough was baptized**